A Shot in the Dark

The Taming of Venus

For Sarah

ORCHARD BOOKS
96 Leonard Street, London EC2A 4XD
Orchard Books Australia
14 Mars Road, Lane Cove, NSW 2066
This text was first published in Great Britain in the form of
a gift collection called *The Orchard Book of Roman Myths*,
illustrated by Emma Chichester Clark in 1999.
This edition first published in hardback in Great Britain in 2000
First paperback publication 2001
Text © Geraldine McCaughrean 1999
Illustrations © Tony Ross 2000
The rights of Geraldine McCaughrean to be identified as the author and
Tony Ross as the illustrator of this work have been asserted by them in
accordance with the Copyright, Designs, and Patents Act, 1988.
ISBN 1 84121 889 8 (hardback)
ISBN 1 84121 526 0 (paperback)
1 3 5 7 9 10 8 6 4 2 (hardback)
1 3 5 7 9 10 8 6 4 2 (paperback)
A CIP catalogue record for this book is available
from the British Library.
Printed in Great Britain

A SHOT IN THE DARK

THE TAMING OF VENUS

GERALDINE MCCAUGHREAN
ILLUSTRATED BY TONY ROSS

 ORCHARD BOOKS

A Shot in the Dark

No brother and sister could have been more different than Apollo and Diana. For Apollo had mastery over the sun and was hot-blooded and passionate. His sister, like the moon she mastered, was all coldness and pallor. Whereas Apollo chased any and every female, Diana had no interest in men, no patience with Love. Though nightly she kissed the shepherd Endymion at the portals of dawn, she had no wish for him to wake and return her kisses.

"I shall never marry," she told her
father, and Jupiter dared not contradict her,
for which of the Immortals would want
such a coldly solitary bride? He allowed
her to remain single, accompanied only by
her train of unmarried nymphs. Beating the
night forests with flails of moonlight, they
nightly set the game birds flying, the red
stags running. Diana was content to hunt,
and she hunted better than any man.

There were seven sisters called the Pleiades among her followers, each as pretty as the other. They loved their mistress and had no wish to marry. What is more, they knew the penalty if they so much as smiled at a man while in the service of the virgin goddess.

So when Orion the Hunter caught sight
of them one day, and came after them,
intrigued by their prettiness, the seven fled
him as they would a bear.

Orion was very like a bear – the great
bulk of his shoulders, his mop of black
hair. He was immensely tall, built on the
scale of a god – a giant almost – and,
being a hunter, he was quick on his feet.

The girls had to run their hardest to stay ahead of him. Their fright and flight upset Orion – he meant them no harm – so he ran all the faster, calling for them to stop: "Don't be afraid! Don't run away!"

But the girls kept running: "Save us, mistress! Save us!"

As Orion's outstretched fingers
brushed flying hair, the seven outran the
very crest of a hill, planting their little feet
in the springy black turf of the night sky.
Staring after them in astonishment, he
watched the Pleiades diminish to the size
of children, of flowers, of flower petals,
as they ran into the distant dark.

So that was where Orion stood when Diana first saw him. Full of rage, fully intending to turn him into some blighted tree or hideous beast, she sprinted up to him, hands spread to make magic. But her glare turned to blushes as he smiled at her.

She saw, for the first time, this matchless piece of mankind. With his bow across his back, his great swordbelt cinched low about his hips, and his face flushed from running, here stood the greatest living hunter, a match for even the immortal huntress. His dog Sirius ran up, panting and grinning, and plunged his nose into her hand, snuffing the familiar scent of hunting.

As Orion smiled at Diana, all thought of the seven sisters slipped from his mind, and he loved Diana as instantly and completely as she loved him. They fell into step together, no words spoken, no words needed. The Moon goddess had found her mate. Orion's dog whimpered a little at being left behind unnoticed, then ran to catch up.

Day and night the two hunted together, and often the moon remained bright in the sky long after the sun was up.

The sun. Golden chariot of Diana's brother.

Apollo drove at breakneck speed
across the blue fields of day, eagle-eyed,
watching every man and beast, every right
and wrong, every house and temple and
trickling stream. He ploughed up the
shadows with blades of sunlight so as to
see into every cranny. No secret stayed
hidden long from Apollo: no pretty face,
dappled deer, no shady trickery, no lovers'
tryst. He was brash and inquisitive,
jealous of any happiness that was not his.
He was arrogant and vain, too, and as
spiteful as sunlight in a mirror.

When he saw Diana and Orion together, he laughed with disbelief at first, then with scorn. "What's this? My haughty sister who claims to despise all men so utterly? Holding hands with a mortal? What would our father Jupiter say, who granted you permission to stay single?" A hot, nagging pain just below his ribs made Apollo grind his teeth. Too proud to recognise the pangs of jealousy, he called it outrage. "You must be taught a lesson, sister. You must learn not to say one thing and do another!"

So Apollo kept watch until Diana was alone and walking on the foothills of Heaven. She was too thoughtful and happy even to quarrel with her brother when he chanced along in his loud yellow tunic and golden sandals.

"Our father was talking this morning of a contest among the gods," said Apollo blithely. "An Olympiad for Olympians. I said I would win every laurel."

"You might," Diana conceded generously. "Except for archery, of course."

"Archery? Why?
Who could beat me at
archery? Boy Cupid?"

"I could, naturally."
Diana folded her arms.

"You? Beat me? Huh!"
Diana frowned and
stamped one foot.
"Everyone knows I am
the best bar one—" She broke off, thinking
better of naming Orion. He was her dear

secret. "Bar none,"
she corrected herself.

"Huh!" snorted
Apollo. "Why, with
better light I could
shoot that speck in the
ocean and sink it." He
pointed out across a sea
purpling in the twilight.

Far, far out, halfway to the horizon, a tiny dark speck bobbed on the waves: a seagull or a piece of driftwood.

"And I say I could hit it even in this light!" retorted Diana. "I can hit black boar in thickets of ebony at midnight." Stringing her bow in one smooth movement, Diana aimed an arrow at the distant fleck on the ocean...

✳   ✳   ✳

Out beneath the first stars of evening,
his dark hair spreading out from his head,
Orion let the cool salt ocean wash away
the dust and sweat of the day. He imagined
swimming in the navy sky, where stars
floated like little white fish and the Milky
Way made a reef of white water. He
thought of Diana, lovely Diana – of her
brown fingers on the bowstring, of her
soft footfall among the forest twigs...

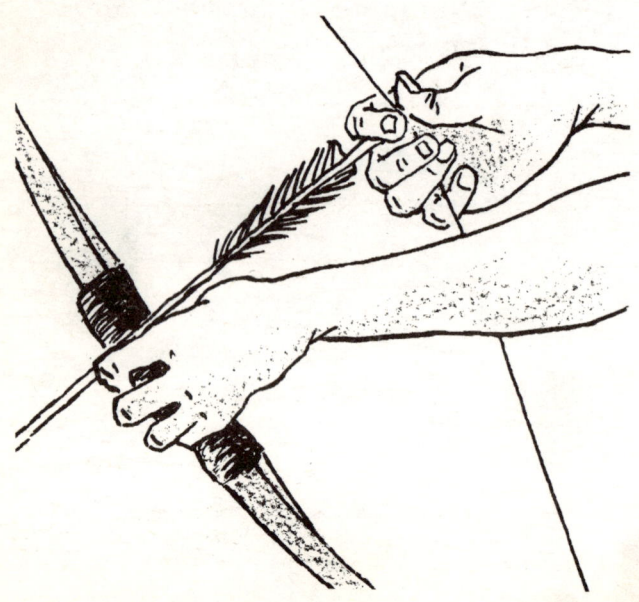

There was a thrumming
hum in the purpling air,
but he did not think
'arrows', did not think
'death'. He thought
a shooting star must
be falling towards
him out of
the sky...

When the arrow struck him in the
throat, his dark eyes widened momentarily
and he threw back his head, so that he
glimpsed the seven little sisters, small as
flower petals, huddling together at the far
end of Night. Then the sea closed over his
face, and the next wave rolled him over to
. float face down and dead.

"I shall never forgive you, Apollo," said Diana when she found out what she had done. Her brother sniggered and shrugged, but he found that the pain beneath his ribs had grown to an ache of regret. He had never seen his sister's face so ashy pale, never seen tears fall so fast from a face. "I swear I shall never forgive you," she said.

Apollo tossed his head with an arrogant, what-do-I-care swagger, and whipped his chariot horses to a gallop.

But when he passed through the gates of sunset and glanced back at the night, he saw his sister dragging her lover behind

her chariot like a victorious warrior dragging a vanquished opponent. She dragged Orion's body behind her silver chariot, up into the sky, while the dog Sirius ran howling behind.

At the sky's zenith, she let Orion go, and his great form dissolved into fragments of light, expanding larger and larger until a starlight giant stood on the fields of night. His dog, too, she exploded into stars.

"You must keep him company now,"
Diana told Sirius. "Help him to watch
over the Earth from now till the stars
blow away." Pausing only to buckle
round Orion's hips a new swordbelt of
stars, she whipped up her own chariot
and drove on towards dawn.

The seven sisters joined hands and danced in a ring to think that, now the danger was passed, Diana would fetch them down again to rejoin her train. But though they called out to her, they were too far off to make her hear, and Diana's mind was fixed on other things.

They are there even now, the seven sisters, the Pleiades. So, too, is Orion the Hunter, though he never glances their way. Nor does he even turn his head to see the

Moon drive by. There is no heart beating, you see, in the hollow expanse of his chest. He is a constellation, untroubled by love or loneliness, heat or cold, trickery or sorrow. And he cuts such a gigantic figure, framed by Infinity, that Apollo, driving by in his golden chariot, looks no bigger than a bee buzzing through the grass at his feet.

THE TAMING OF VENUS

Venus came in on the roll of a wave – on a chariot of blue water, canopied by the following wave as it curled over her head. She was sea spray; she was flesh-pale as sea spray. In the breaking of the wave she became alive, and as the wave withdrew it left Venus standing naked on the beach. Born where sea and sky kiss, Venus was all Love.

The moment the gods saw her, they began to woo her – Mars and Mercury, Apollo and Neptune. So the King of the Gods, to save a feud in Heaven, declared that Venus must marry at once. She would marry Vulcan, he said.

Poor, deformed Vulcan, Blacksmith of the Gods, was lame and ugly and soot-stained from the fires of his forges. But when he heard the news, his heart beat louder and faster than his own blacksmith's hammer.

"*Marry Vulcan?* Never! I would sooner live single than marry that lump of ugliness!" declared Venus.

But there was no defying the will of
the king. The sight of exquisite Venus
alongside her dwarfish bridegroom made
the gods rock with laughter. Vulcan felt
that laughter like sparks from his anvil:
it burned him to the quick. Worse still
was the look of disgust in
his bride's eyes, for he
adored her and knew
he would never have
his love returned.

Sure enough, as soon as Vulcan's back was turned, Venus broke all her wedding vows. She went in search of Mars – handsome, surly god of war, and to him she gave all the kisses she would not give her ugly husband.

Apollo saw the two together as he drove his chariot sun across the linseed blue sky. Partly out of jealousy, partly out of spite, he drove directly to the blacksmith's forge and told him: "Your wife is with Mars, Vulcan. Obviously she prefers his company to yours."

Vulcan's hammer crashed down and his anvil cracked from end to end. Hastily Apollo withdrew, sniggering at the sound of Vulcan's tears hissing on to the forge.

Now, Vulcan was a craftsman – an artist, a genius. Though his head was ugly, the brain inside it was ingenious. He set about forging a net made of steel chains so fine that they were all but invisible, so strong they could snare and hold a fleet of crocodiles.

This net he strung up in the branches of a tree, stretching it out like a spider's web over the place where Venus and Mars liked to sit. Then he sat in the tree and waited.

As the lovers met and kissed and whispered together, Vulcan let the net drop. Mars and Venus lay tangled like two chickens in a string bag, and no amount of struggling or cursing or magic could free them.

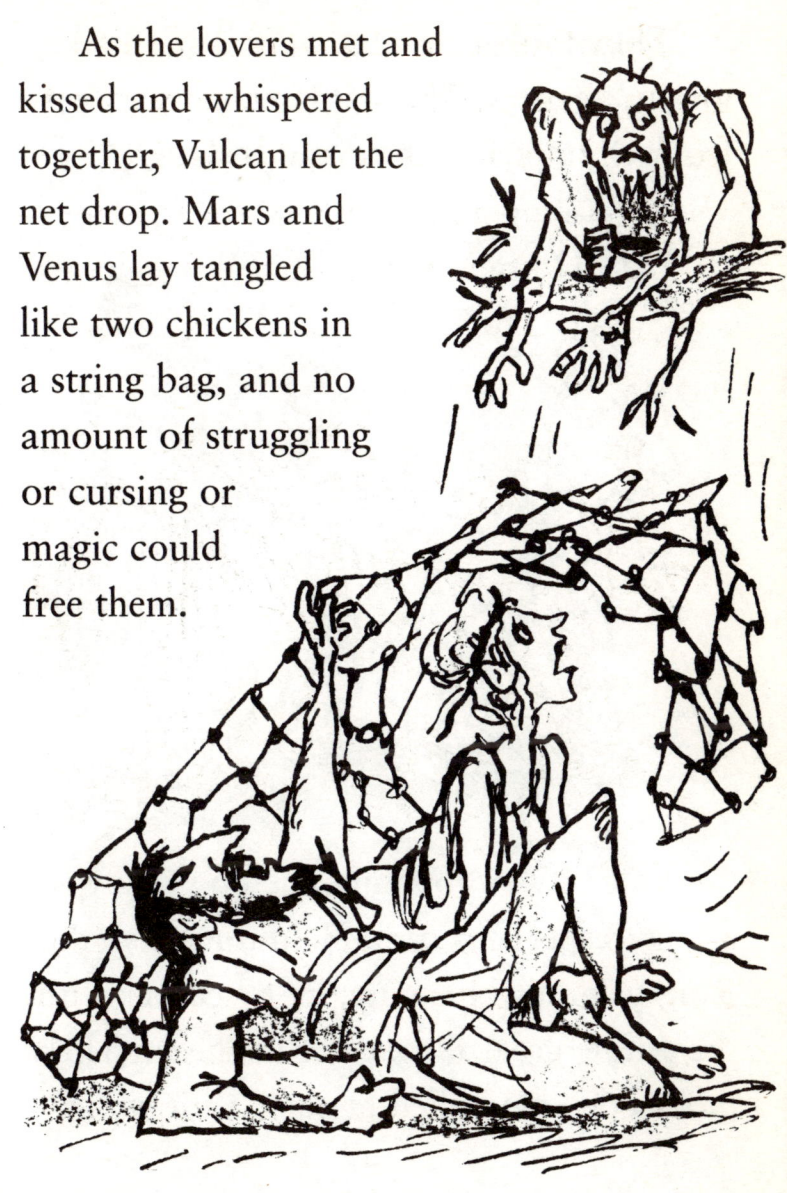

They looked so absurd and shouted so loudly, that the gods came running down from Olympus to stare and to laugh.

Vulcan was content. The gods showed a new respect for him. He did not ask the King to punish his wife: he loved her with the whole great furnace of his heart. The other gods marvelled at such a forgiving nature…but ungrateful Venus only tossed her head, still haughty, still contemptuous.

"What punishment could be worse than to be married to the ugliest man in Heaven?" she said, driving another shard of pain through Vulcan's broken heart.

Perhaps her father heard her and thought she needed to be taught a lesson. Or perhaps it was simply Fate. But Venus soon regretted her words. For she found herself head over heels in love, and not with any handsome god, not with any cupbearer or woodland spirit – not even with her ugly husband. No, Venus fell in love with a *mortal man*.

Anchises of Troy seemed to her more beautiful than golden-haired Apollo or surly, muscular Mars. She wept and bewailed her foolishness – a goddess in love with a mortal! – but could no more break free than if chains of steel bound her to Anchises.

"Swear you will never tell anyone about us – not anyone!" she begged him. "Swear to me you will never boast that you conquered the goddess of love. Swear to me, my love, oh my love!"

Anchises swore, but it was a hard promise to keep – especially when Venus bore him a son – Aeneas. "May I not even tell the boy his mother's name?" he pleaded.

"Never! Never! Or by this hand, it will be the last word you speak. I swear, Anchises, if you ever break your promise, you will die in the instant!" Even as she said it, Venus wished it unsaid, for now she would be afraid every moment, in case Anchises broke his word and died and she had to live everlastingly without him.

Anchises was not a proud or boastful man, but a hundred times a day he was tempted to break his promise. When his son asked, "Who is my mother? Why is she not here in the house, baking bread like all the other mothers? Did she die? Why do you never speak of her? What was her name, at least?"

Finally Aeneas learned that no amount of asking would ever gain him an answer. It seemed to matter less as he grew older. Venus watched over her son secretly, from the slopes of Heaven and sent him a Trojan wife and a son of his own to love.

But even she was powerless to prevent what happened next.

Mars brought war to the city of Troy.

Over the seas came the Greeks, and laid siege to the City of Horses. They fired their arrows into the streets; they challenged the young men of Troy to fight in mortal combat on the shores of the sea.

"Forbid this, Father! Call Mars off! Stop the war!" cried Venus, kneeling before the King of the Gods.

"I commanded it," answered the King. "The people of Earth have grown noisy and troublesome. Ten years of war will thin them out like seedlings and leave only the strongest alive." He held out his cup for nectar. A drop spilled on his finger. "Ganymede? Do you tremble, boy?"

"But my city! I was born in Troy!" cried the little Cupbearer to the Gods. "Will Troy win the war?"

The King strummed his lips; he had
not thought so far ahead. "If Troy falls, its
spirit will live on – somehow, somewhere.
This I swear." And he laid a soothing
hand on Ganymede's curly hair.

Venus could say nothing, without
betraying her shameful secret.

She could only sit and watch Troy besieged, Troy captured, Troy burning. Must her beloved Anchises and Aeneas die in flames? Zeus's words came back to her: "*Troy's spirit will live on – somehow, somewhere.*" Well, then, let it live on in her boy, Aeneas!

Dipping her face into the smoke of the burning city, Venus whispered, "Run, Aeneas! *Run!*"